MW00652793

# THE
# SEVEN
# SPIRITUAL
# LAWS
## OF
# MAKING
# BIG BUCKS

# THE
# SEVEN
# SPIRITUAL
# LAWS
## OF
# MAKING
# BIG BUCKS

࿔

A PRACTICAL GUIDE
TO THE SELF-RIGHTEOUS AMASSING
*of* AN OBSCENE FORTUNE

## DEEPOCKETS CHOKYA

RGE PUBLISHING

**The Seven Spiritual Laws
of Making Big Bucks**
© 1998 RGE Publishing

All rights reserved. No part of this book may be reproduced or transmitted in any form or by any means, electronic or mechanical, except by a reviewer who may quote brief passages in a review to be printed in a magazine or newspaper, without permission in writing from the publisher. This is a parody of a popular book. It is intended to be humorous. It is a joke, nothing more, nothing less. Any resemblance to any person, living or dead — other than the best-selling author who is obviously being satirized herein — is purely coincidental. Despite our humorous intent, we heartily encourage that esteemed author to consider suing us for libel, slander, defamation of character, plagiarism, invasion of privacy, and industrial espionage, as the publicity generated would greatly enhance our sales. Oh yes, and Jimmy Swaggart never made the statement attributed to him on page 44, at least not in so few words.

Published by: **RGE Publishing**

414 Santa Clara Avenue
Oakland CA 94610
(510) 465-6452
FAX: (510) 652-4330
Web site: www.rge21.com
e-mail: books@rge21.com

First Edition

1 2 3 4 5 6 7 8 9 10

ISBN 0-910575-07-X

You are what your deep, driving desire is.

As your desire is, so is your will.

As your will is, so is your deed.

As your deed is, so is your ability

to reap the tax benefits of being a slumlord.

— *Bompshibomp Upanishad XII.6.9*

# CONTENTS

# ACKNOWLEDGMENTS

I would like to express my love and gratitude to the following people:

Not one lonely soul.

I wrote this book.

Not my mother.

Not my father.

Not any of my ex-wives.

Not my kids.

Not one of my so-called friends.

As a matter of fact, all of the above have attempted throughout my life to discourage me from doing anything worthwhile by their constant complaining, moping, bitching and whining.

I hate whiners.

As far as I'm concerned, they can all take a flying leap.

And I'm certainly not going to dedicate this book to the publisher's nerdy editorial staff, whose sole claim to fame is the ability to run a spell-check program in WordPerfect.

There's not one person on this planet I want to thank. So, screw you all.

And if you follow the advice in this book, you may be lucky enough to turn into a real son-of-a-bitch like me. And someday, you can write your own how-to-get-rich-quick book.

And quite honestly, I won't expect you to thank me for "inspiring" you, because if you do stick my name anywhere in your plagiaristic book, you'll pay me a handsome royalty or I'll sue your ass, you unoriginal moron.

# INTRODUCTION

**A**lthough this book is titled *The Seven Spiritual Laws of Making Big Bucks,* it could also be called *Debbie Does the Department of the Treasury.* In fact, it might even sell better if there were some kind of dirty sexual reference in the title because cheap smut is just one of the many ways a real bastard can make a bundle in this sicko world.

But since smut is just one small (but fun!) facet of how to clean up, and I want to provide you with a more well-rounded education in how to wallow in wealth, I'll save "Debbie" for a future get-rich-quick scheme. Once you understand the fundamentals of wealth-wallowing, your existence on this planet will cease to be the insipid soap opera you currently call your life, and shall become a grand drama of adventure, intrigue and romance.

Step back and look at your life. If you're like most people, you work a dull job that you hate, day in and day out, kissing up to obnoxious, power-mad authority figures who look at you and treat you like a bothersome insect, who lord their position over you 8 to 10 hours per day, 5 days per week, 50 weeks per year. And after each frustrating, humiliating day at work, you go home to your spouse, who despises you for your shameful, insipid lifestyle, berates you, tears you down, and generally makes your home life a living hell.

Your ungrateful, delinquent children steal money from your wallet, never stop screeching and fighting, are ashamed to be seen with you in front of their friends, and make you wish you had sold them to the gypsies when they were squalling infants. And you would have sold them to the gypsies had there ever been any gypsies passing through your neighborhood. Unfortunately, the only itinerants you ever see are the local Jehovah's Witnesses.

The tacky pasteboard box you call your home is a financial prison that eats your paycheck before you've even collected it. And the only hope you possess for happiness is the handful of lottery tickets you buy each Friday at the local 7-11 with the few remnants of your meager paycheck that haven't yet disappeared to angry bill collectors. These thugs with bad teeth and brass knuckles lurk in the shadows of your nightmares, ready to repossess your worthless car and put a lien on your empty bank accounts should you be late one more time on the payment for something you bought years ago which you no longer possess. And you call this dead-end, utterly boring excuse for breathing, your "life."

ॐ    ॐ    ॐ

Before defining the *Seven Spiritual Laws of Making Big Bucks,* let us spell out exactly what we mean by "law." Law is the process by which something somebody else has becomes your property, the process by which the observer becomes the owner, the process by which the dreamer makes life a nightmare for everyone else.

All that exists in creation is but illusion, a creation of the One Mind. No one can own illusion. It just is.

But since the masses of humanity understand nothing of spiritual evolution, they believe all this stuff is real, and they firmly believe in the concepts of possession and ownership. What a bunch of unevolved idiots!

You, however, knowing the true illusory nature of all you perceive, can use the astounding ignorance of the masses to your benefit. The trick is to realize that you can't actually own anything — it's all illusion; there is really nothing to own. But if you can make the dolts who populate this planet believe you own something, then for all intents and purposes in this life, it's yours.

For example, when I give a seminar on spiritual evolution, I charge eight hundred bucks a head. The fact that I say nothing in this seminar that cannot be purchased in one of my many books — which are already overpriced at $9.95 — matters not. If I say the seminar costs $800, then that's what people pay, *and believe they ought to pay.* Since the whole concept of dollar value is illusory in the first place, and I'm the only one in the convention hall with brains enough to know this, then I get to make the value rules. It's that simple!

And consider how people give me this $800 for the privilege of sitting in a stuffy Holiday Inn conference room where I flap my jaw for an hour and a half. Do they come with $800 worth of gold or silver, or even apples or toasters or tickets to baseball games, or anything of real value? No. Nothing of real value changes hands. A few many bring small scraps of wrinkled green paper that supposedly *represent* $800 worth of U.S. currency — but we all know what the national debt is; this paper isn't worth a handful of dirt in reality.

Most attendees, however, don't even bring wrinkled paper; they arrive with a little plastic card that gets electronically "scanned" — a process by which a computer at my bank instructs a computer at their bank to transfer $800 in electronic blips from their balance sheet to mine! That's it!

Is it real?

Of course not. They've given me nothing of value, and I've taken nothing of value. But the fact is they believe they've given me $800, and what's more, *their bank* believes they've given me $800; and most importantly of all, *my bank* believes the same lie! They are all under the illusion that I have collected $800 each from 650 different new age nincompoops, and at the end of the day, my bank balance reads more than half a million bucks higher than when the day began!

Do the math, buster! What an illusion!

This, then, is the eternal dance of life. Supposedly real stuff, which is actually illusory, gets divvied up among lost souls who believe it to be real. Once you realize, however, that everything in creation flows within the Field of Pure Greed, you can manifest any amount of this illusory stuff to flow directly into your illusory pockets! While others bump into walls searching for their identities, a purpose to life, a fulfilling job, a meaningful relationship, social stature, political freedom, blah, blah, blah — you slowly clean them all out for everything they're worth, and never look back.

*The Seven Spiritual Laws of Making Big Bucks* are actually the whole process of divinity in motion, and when you get that motion moving in your direction, you're rich!

So, let's get on with it. Let's see how you can use the Laws of the Universe to get rich like me.

# ❧ 1 ❧
# THE LAW
# OF PURE GREED

*The source of all creation is Pure Greed. That is why our One True Self has created the entire universe in the first place. Eternity, without toys, is boring as hell. Greed runs the show, and when we realize this, we align with the almighty power that manifests everything, and we rake in the loot. It's that simple.*

❦

*In the beginning*
*There was neither wealth nor poverty,*
*All this universe was but a waste of time.*

*The One breathed, for some unknown reason,*
*And in the stillness of nonexistence,*
*Opened a Swiss bank account.*

> *Hymn of Creation*
> — *Big Veda and the Sutrazettes*

The first spiritual law of making big bucks is the *Law of Pure Greed.* This law is based on the fact that we are, in our essential state, really heartless bastards. Pure heartlessness is pure greed; it is the essence of all of creation. As our capacity for greed is infinite — you can never have too much! — it also leads to unlimited joy and satisfaction. Other attributes of Pure Greed are uncontrolled gluttony, shameless lust, fame, fortune, political clout, powerful underworld connections, and social prominence. This is all part of our essential nature — Pure Greed.

Once you discover greed to be your essential nature and you know who you really are, you will have the ability to fulfill every dream, every fantasy, every sick desire, every perverse reverie that you have, because you will be one with the eternal possibility, the unlimited potential of all that was, is and will be. *The Law of Pure Greed* could also be called *The Law of Vindication* because underlying the act of acquiring everything you want to own is the joyous satisfaction that comes from knowing that you are getting back everything that is rightfully yours. After all, you are One with the Creator. The Field of Pure Greed is your own Self, and the more you experience your true divine nature as the One True Cosmic Bastard, the closer you are to the eternal truth of creation itself.

The experience of the true Self, or "self-righteousness," means that no matter how cruel and despicable we may appear to others, we really don't give a shit. Is it our problem if their consciousness is so Neanderthal that they believe all these illusory material possessions to be real and valuable?

Sorry, buddy, it's not my problem.

Since when do I have to feel guilty about owning illusions? Take a hike, numskull! If we constantly do things for the approval of others, we subtract ourselves from our essential nature. This is because greediness is never approved of by those who are victimized by it. When we seek the approval of others for our actions, we condemn ourselves to the same dreary lives as the pathetic, unenlightened souls who surround us. Instead of seeking the approval of others, we should take courage in the prayer of the Tibetan monk, Lo Blo, as he sold the village children into slavery:

*These are but innocent children,*
*Trusting,*
*Vulnerable,*
*The crowning beauty of creation.*
*So fork over the cash*
*and I'll hit the road.*

The intense need for the approval of others is a need that is based on fear. To seek approval is to live in fear, to be a spineless, powerless wimp. When we relinquish the need for the approval of others, based on our true self-righteous nature, we experience true power, true happiness, and a sense of oneness with all of creation.

Your true Self is immune to all criticism, unfearful of any challenge, for you have the money to hire the best and slimiest lawyers. You are beneath no one, no matter how disgusting you are, no matter what civil laws you break, no matter who you step on in your rise to sainthood, no matter what "crimes of nature" you may be accused of by the unenlightened. You shall know in your heart that you are following your true nature, and that all who oppose you are fearful little weaklings with empty lives and empty wallets.

That is the essential difference between *self-righteousness* and *righteousness*. With self-righteousness, you are immune to the opinions and judgments of others. You have no fear, no boundaries on your behavior, and not one iota of respect for anything anyone else says. And only through self-righteousness can you realize the abundant fruits of the universe available to you through the *Law of Pure Greed*.

It does happen on occasion that ignorant, unevolved, righteous people acquire positions of power. We have all seen dopey do-gooders whose aims appear unselfish rise in stature and social position. But this is never true power, nor does it last. Ultimately, these jerks are at odds with the Universe, and their fragile success will surely be punctured, their egos deflated, their financial gains lost in the end.

Self-righteous power, on the other hand, always grows. It magnetizes other greedy people to you, and through them, more and more power and money flow in your direction. Your power is the true power of Universal Truth — and that, my friend, is Pure Greed.

How can we apply the *Law of Pure Greed,* the field of all wealth and abundance, to our lives? If you want to enjoy the immense pleasure of having everything you want, and lording it over others who do your bidding like common servants, then you must learn to access this law for your benefit. One way to access the Law is through the daily practice of silence and meditation, while cultivating unbridled ruthlessness. Through this process, you will achieve that state reverently regarded by the mystics of all ages as a *bad attitude*.

Life is a kick in the head. The first of the four noble truths as taught by Buddha is that *life is suffering.* Most people are forever bitching and moaning about their sorry lot. They're whiners.

By practicing meditation, however, we silently stew in the frustrating juices of our pathetic lives; and it is this stewing process which provides us with the impetus to rise above the human condition.

Set aside a little time each day to silently experience the disgusting crap happening all around you. If you can just turn off the TV and the radio, and shut up for half an hour each evening, you will be amazed at the powerful rage that begins to build inside you. And every once in a while, you should experience this meditative silence for an extended period of time — a whole day, or two days, or even a full week. Just go check in to a Motel Six, tell no one where you are, and stare at the walls for a few days. Don't turn on the TV or the radio. Don't read the paper. Just sit and stare like an idiot at the peeling wallpaper and listen to the nerve-wracking, irritating drone of the freeway traffic outside.

What happens when you meditate like this? Initially, your internal dialogue really cranks up. You'll remember embarrassing shit you haven't thought about for years — people who shafted you one way or another, catastrophes that have befallen you, shameful childhood incidents. All the garbage of life you've been repressing rises to the top.

But stick with it. Stew in it. After a while, the mind gives up, realizing there is no point in whining about this crap, and you will begin to develop that ruthless *bad attitude* that will allow you to quit your mental bitching and access the *Law of Pure Greed.*

In the third spiritual law, the *Law of Helping Others to Reap Their Bad Karma,* you will see how your bad attitude and ruthless actions can actually help others to ultimately achieve enlightenment through being ripped off by you. But before you can help others to do this, you must cultivate a bad attitude well beyond the simpering dissatisfaction of the masses. You need a powerful bad attitude, an attitude so bad that you could commit virtually any atrocity imaginable with a smile on your face, provided it puts a few more bucks into your pocket.

Imagine throwing a pebble into a still pond, then watching the ripples. This is similar to the effect of whining, a few moments of barely discernible waves on the surface of life. Five minutes later, it's a faint memory.

Now imagine throwing the Empire State Building into the Okefenokee Swamp. Quite a catastrophe. Think of all those lawyers and CPA's in their soiled three-piece suits, buried in muck and bricks and splintered glass. Dazed alligators roaming through three states, feasting on household pets named Fluffy and Bowser and Tweetie, all nauseated into submission by swamp gas. Anyone owning stock in the Red Cross becomes an overnight millionaire. This is how cultivating ruthlessness compares to whining.

Another way to access the Field of Pure Greed is through the practice of *prejudgment*. Normally, we continually judge things throughout each day as good or bad, weighing how the various factors involved affect our lives. This constant judgment process takes a lot of energy and wastes a lot of time. It disturbs the process of silent stewing that leads to true ruthless action.

But if you are honest with yourself, you will realize that virtually everything that happens to you is a kick in the head. Each moment you live, you are one moment closer to your death. Each minute that passes, you owe another few bucks in federal taxes to an ineffectual government that continues to go deeper in debt.

Nothing good ever happens, so why waste your time and energy in this constant process of judgment? If you simply prejudge everything as just another pain in the ass, before it even occurs, you free your consciousness to always take the appropriate ruthless response, without hesitation.

There is a prayer in *A Course in Disgust* that states, "Today I shall hate everything that occurs." Hatred creates silent stewing in your mind. Begin each day with this prayer and repeat it to yourself throughout each day, and ruthless action will become second nature to you.

Any time you catch yourself judging something that occurs in your life, stop and remember this prayer. If someone comes up and hands you a flower, do not sit and wonder whether this person may have good intentions or is merely trying to get something out of you. In your heart, you know the answer. Why waste your energy judging? Simply smile at this person who comes bearing this lovely gift, and nod a warm thank you, all the while thinking, "You little shit, you won't get a goddamn thing out of me. I know you're up to something, you worm. Your ass is grass; I'll take you for everything you're worth."

If practicing prejudgment throughout the whole day, every day, seems too difficult, then say to yourself: "For the next two hours, I will judge nothing, but will hate everything and everyone equally," or "For the next one hour, I will practice prejudgment." Then you may extend the time gradually.

Through your silence, meditation, and prejudgment, you will access the first law, the *Law of Pure Greed.* Once you begin this process, you may add another component to this practice, and that is spending time in frivolous litigation with anyone who crosses your path. It's not necessary that you carry through with a legal action against your enemies; merely threatening litigation, as if you were dead serious about it, is enough of a disturbance in most people's lives that you will feel a unity with all of life — the forests, the mountains, the lawyers — and this connection with nature's intelligence and nastiness will also help you to access the Field of Pure Greed.

You must learn to get in touch with your innermost essence, which is beyond your puny ego. It knows no fear, is absolutely reckless, immune to all criticism — in fact, welcomes criticism, as criticism often leads to arguments which always bring out the worst in people. Your true essence is beneath no one, superior to the disillusioned dolts who populate this sphere, steeped in power, unpredictability, and carelessness about the feelings of others.

Access to your true essence will also give you insight into your relationships with others, since every relationship you have is like a mirror reflection of your relationship with yourself. For example, if you hate your job and you're going nowhere, despite all the disgusting kissing up you do to your despicable bosses and managers, this is merely a reflection of who you are inside yourself — a spineless turd with no real concern for anything other than money and power. Yet you adamantly refuse to admit this truth to yourself consciously.

Ask yourself this: Do you really give a flying fuck if the company you work for produces anything of real value for its customers? If you're working for Liggett and Myers, the answer is obvious. But most of us aren't fortunate enough to work for the tobacco companies; we work for hypocritical businesses that insist they offer truly valuable products and services to people — food, clothing, shelter, entertainment, hardware, software, health care, insurance, education, knowledge, hope, security...

What a crock.

Name any business and consider what they're really doing — buying low, selling high, and taking their chunk out of the middle. Every business will buy as low as it can and sell as high as it can, so that that middle chunk it stuffs into its own greedy pockets is all the bigger. The only difference between you and Liggett & Myers is that you don't own a few hundred thousand acres of tobacco plants.

As you gain more and more access to your true nature, you will spontaneously get creative impulses because the Field of Pure Greed is also the field of infinite creativity. Franz Kafka, the Austrian writer who died drunk in a gutter, once said: "I am a cockroach." Too bad he wasted his life writing pointless short stories and maudlin poems. Had he been able to accept that revelation, he may have gone into advertising, or pornography, or something that would have put a little money into his bank account.

The wealth of the universe is an expression of the creative mind of nature. The more you tune into nature, the more you will tune into your own essence. Now, if I tell you to look at the cockroaches and vultures and sewer rats to find the essence of nature and the essence of your true self, you may accuse me of stacking the deck. You may counter, "But what of the graceful butterfly or the lovely morning dove whose beautiful song greets each day? Is this dove not also the creation of Nature?"

You sappy, romantic asshole. You probably waste your afternoons pining over TV soap operas. You are truly pathetic.

Let's consider that lovely morning dove just a bit deeper — say about half an inch deeper. Slice that sucker open and what do you find? Blood and guts and partially digested insects. That morning dove may be a sweet and lovely song to you, but it's a winged horror factory to the local arthropod population, including that pretty little butterfly. Look at the claws on that "harmless" little birdie. How'd you like to see a set of talons like that, magnified a hundredfold, with one of those toenails punctured into your abdomen, while that razor-sharp beak works away at your flesh, unconcerned with your screams or your writhing? It doesn't even have the decency to kill you first, to put you out of your misery. Why should it care about your pain? It's hungry, that's all. And if you're a bug, you're food.

Morning dove indeed. When we look to the morning dove, really look at its essence, we learn the same lesson we learn from the cockroach and the sewer rat. Nothing more, nothing less. Life is hungry. Life is ruthless. And the essence of existence is Pure Greed. All of life eats, and all of life is ultimately eaten. This paradoxical coexistence of opposites — eater and eaten — is central to your understanding of, and access to, the Field of Pure Greed.

THE LAW OF PURE GREED

When you finally acknowledge to yourself this horror that life is, you align yourself with the universe, and you become at peace with yourself and all of creation, knowing yourself to be — like the sweet and lovely morning dove — hungry, greedy, powerful and heartless.

# APPLYING THE
# LAW OF PURE GREED

I will put the *Law of Pure Greed* into effect by making a commitment to take the following steps:

(1) I will get in touch with the Field of Pure Greed by taking time each day to be silent, to sit alone and meditate for at least thirty minutes, or until I feel my ruthless hatred for all of existence arise in my soul.

(2) I will take some time each day to commune with lawyers as I consider what threats of litigation I might make in order to disrupt the peaceful lives of those whom I decide to lord my power over.

(3) I will continually practice prejudgment, beginning each day with the proclamation: "Today, I will hate everything that occurs and everyone who has the nerve to cross my path," and throughout the day, I will remind myself to cut no one any slack.

# 2

# THE LAW
# OF TAKING

*The universe operates through dynamic
exchange. Ripping off and being ripped off
are different aspects of the flow of
energy in the universe.
And in our greediness to take that which we
want, we keep the abundance of the universe
flowing into our own pockets.*

*I am you, and you are me.*
*He is she, and she is that.*
*That is this, and this is mine.*
*So get your hands off it.*

— *Kahlil Pastafazuli*

The second spiritual law of making big bucks is the *Law of Taking.* This law could also be called the *Law of Taking and Being Taken From,* because you can bet your ass if you've got more than others, they'll be trying their damnedest to even up the score.

We need only look to nature to see examples of this. Take six hungry dogs and toss them five big juicy T-bones. You've got yourself a dog fight. And you can bet that the biggest and meanest dog will end up with two bones, or even three, and the smallest, most cowardly mutts will be run off whimpering with their tails between their legs, probably dripping blood from their chewed up ears.

In the springtime, it's rutting season in the breathtaking Canadian Rockies, and the Great Elks clash over the right to mate with the females of the herd. The violent battle sometimes goes on for days, as the horny young bucks try to usurp the reigning stud's alpha position.

Whether we look at dogs or elks or vultures or hyenas, we see nature in all her glory — a never-ending celebration of greed, lust, violence and bad attitudes. Of all the animals on earth, however, only man has become so detached from his true nature that instead of trying to get everything he can, he wastes his time pining over lost loves, worrying himself sick over the despicable details of his human relationships, kissing ass whenever some so-called authority figure bends over in front of him, and generally becomes a pathetic, depressed piece of limp protoplasm that drudges through each boring day in shame and embarrassment, spending his so-called "leisure" time hunched in front of the boob tube with a beer in one hand and a remote control in the other.

We have forgotten that it is our nature to take. Everything in this universe is yours for the taking. Look again at the dog. Does he ask of the dogs around him, "Whose bone is this?" Does the young elk ask the reigning stud, "Excuse me, but are those your mates?" When you find your picnic lunch under seige by a swarming ant colony, did the ants first inquire of you, "Pardon me, human, but can you spare a few morsels of your bologna sandwich?"

Dream on, jerk!

It is the nature of nature to take.

And when you take, you give nothing back but a snarl and a threat. And only when you understand your true nature and you live in accordance with the *Law of Taking* will you find peace, happiness and spiritual bliss.

The word "sharing" comes from the Peloponesian root "sharïrê," which means, loosely, "stupid asshole." Sharing is a human concept, foreign to all the rest of nature. Only man, in his mentally deficient subtraction from reality, nurtures this bizarre concept of allowing others to partake of some of his hard-won worldly goods.

Rather than be depressed, however, that you are a pathetic human creature who holds this ridiculous notion of sharing, you should instead rejoice in the knowledge that so many of your kind are oblivious to their own unnatural and stupid behavior. This cosmic truth is your salvation. If you always surround yourself with those who share, you will never want. These saps can be taken for a bundle, never expecting anything in return. It is unnatural to share; it is unnatural to give; only taking is blessed.

You may be saying to yourself right now, "But how can I take things from others when I am such a powerless wimp? I am physically weak, financially depleted, politically impotent, emotionally a wreck. My self-confidence died in my miserable childhood. I am terrified of confrontation. I can take nothing from anyone, for I am a pathetic loser on all counts."

This realization of what a repugnant moron you are is actually the beginning of wisdom. For you are just one breath away from the revelation that you are a cornered rat. Remember the words of Gautama Buddha as he sat beneath the bo tree spitting at the cripples and lepers who passed by begging for alms:

*Consider the cornered rat*
*who sees no direction in which to turn,*
*no escape from his position of fear and horror.*
*He lashes out with teeth and claws*
*in every direction,*
*bloodying and maiming all enemies,*
*and in his blind viciousness*
*delivers himself and becomes like the wind,*
*free and powerful and at one with God.*

So, you're a powerless wimp. How can you take anything from anyone, you wonder, when you're afraid of your own shadow? Unfortunately, you are asking yourself the wrong question! Instead of asking *how* you could possibly take anything from anyone, you must ask yourself, "*Who* can I take something from?"

And the answer, obviously, is from anyone less powerful than you! Look around yourself. Open your eyes. There are always many people less powerful than you. You can filch things from your stupid relatives. You can steal from homeless people, for chrissake!

Unless you happen to be the single least powerful creature on this planet, not only flat broke and homeless, but crippled, incurably diseased, and either blind or too stupid to read these words, you ain't hit bottom yet. And if you ain't hit bottom, you can step on anyone beneath you to begin your journey up. Sure, it will be difficult in the beginning, when those you take things from have so little themselves. It almost seems pointless.

But it's the intention behind your taking that is the important thing — not the dollar value of what you take. If you take anything with joyous ruthlessness, you begin the process of getting the wealth of the universe to flow into your pockets.

A nickel, a single nickel, snatched from the dirty upturned cap of a hungry street musician, can begin the process. It's not important what you take, only that you take. The energy behind your taking always increases many times over.

Practicing the *Law of Taking* is actually very simple: if you want money, take money; if you want power, take power away from someone else; if you want attention, take attention from others; and if you want happiness, make someone miserable. The easiest way to get whatever you want is always to steal it from someone else.

Even the thought of taking something from someone else has the power to affect others. This is because your body, on a cosmic level, is connected to all of creation. When you see someone who has immensely more than you — say some powerful financial baron, or a famous politician or a movie star, or even a king or a queen, someone who lives in a palace encrusted in precious jewels, surrounded by personal servants and body guards — someone like, say, the Pope — do not ignore this powerful person. Do not assume that you could never attain the level of power necessary to take something from such a wealthy and degenerate individual. Your thoughts alone possess great power, and only when you learn to cultivate envy of the rich and powerful, can you ever attain their status yourself.

Remember that many nobodies, once powerless wimps like you, have achieved astounding financial success by becoming or hiring lawyers. They not only take from wealthy individuals, but from corporations and even the government itself. And what is a politician but someone who has learned to take from virtually everybody, big and small alike, with such self-righteous ruthlessness that he does so publicly and proudly?

The best way to put the *Law of Taking* into operation — to start the whole spiritual process of Making Big Bucks — is to make a decision that any time you come into contact with anyone, you will take something from him. It doesn't have to be money, or even something material; it could be a trinket, a cigarette lighter or some silly knickknack from their coffee table. You could even take their peace of mind.

In fact, taking non-material things like this are among the most powerful forms of taking; for they put you into that totally ruthless frame of mind which allows you to access the Field of Pure Greed. Then, when the opportunity to take something of real value arises, you will see it and have the proper bad attitude to seize the moment.

One of the things I was taught as a child, and which I taught my children also, is never to go to anyone's house without getting that person to give you something. You may say, "How can I get my stingy neighbors and relatives to give me anything, when I know how cheap they are, and also that they despise me?" You can get them to give you a cup of coffee, or a glass of water, or just a moment of their time. One worthless moment of attention.

Make a decision to take something, no matter how small, from everywhere you go, from whomever you see. As long as you are taking ruthlessly, your bad attitude will grow, and more and more wealth will come into your life. And the more you get, the more powerful you will become, and the more you will be able to take.

Our true nature is one of wealth and power because the universe itself is abundant and powerful. You lack nothing except the illusion of ownership, and when you access the Field of Pure Greed, through your rigorous practice of the *Law of Taking,* then all the abundant wealth of the universe will flow into your pockets.

# APPLYING THE
# LAW OF TAKING

**I** will put the *Law of Taking* into effect by making a commitment to take the following steps:

(1) Wherever I go and whomever I encounter, I will take something from them. Whether I steal someone's heart or someone's home, I will get something and give nothing in return.

(2) I will also guard my own possessions vigorously. Not one person will get a damn thing out of me, and heaven help anyone who tries. Anything taken from me, I shall vow to get back one hundredfold.

(3) I will make a commitment to maintain my *bad attitude* by continuously focusing with envy on the truly wealthy and powerful people of this world, so that when my opportunity arises to take from them, I will know exactly what I want and exactly how to get it.

# ❧ 3 ❧
# THE LAW
# OF HELPING
# OTHERS TO
# REAP THEIR
# BAD KARMA

*Every action generates a force of energy that returns like a cosmic boomerang. When you choose actions that make life miserable for others, the fact is, they must deserve it. Somebody's got to dole out the bad Karma . . . why not you?*

෨

*Like death and taxes, Karma is inevitable. You are going
to pay the piper in the end. Everything that befalls you is your
own fault. If, by hook or by crook, I steal your house, your car,
your wife, your life savings, it couldn't have happened unless
it was your Karma. You deserve it. No skin off my holy nose.*

*– Swami Ami Rami*

The third spiritual law of making big bucks is the *Law of
Helping Others to Reap Their Bad Karma.* "Karma" is
both action and the shitstorm that follows; it is cause and effect simultaneously. Every action generates a force of energy
that returns like a cosmic boomerang. You can't stop it.

I'm sure you've heard the expression, "What you sow, so
shall you reap." Obviously, if you want to create fabulous
wealth in your life, you must learn to sow the seeds of riches.
Karma is the result of your conscious choice-making. The
choices you have today will mean wealth — or poverty — tomorrow.

Essentially, we are all constantly making choices. At
every moment of our existence, we are choosing the direc-
tions of our lives. Some of these choices we recogn ize as conscious choices, but many are unconscious. If you want to
utilize the *Law of Helping Others to Reap Their Bad Karma* to

make big bucks, you're going to have to break the pattern of making unconscious choices. Pay attention to what you're doing, numskull; it's as simple as that.

Whether you like it or not, every rotten thing that is happening in your life right now is a result of the choices you've made in the past. Unfortunately, you make a lot of choices unconsciously, so you don't really think they're choices — but they are!

For instance, if someone were to insult you, you would probably choose to be offended. If someone were to pay you a compliment, you'd most likely choose to be flattered. But these are your unconscious choices.

If someone insults you, you could choose not to be offended, but to sue his ass. If someone compliments you, you could choose not to be flattered, but to get something out of him.

Unfortunately, your brain isn't conditioned to always think profitably. You respond predictably, and unprofitably, to most everything that occurs in your life, never realizing that these unconsciously driven behaviors ignore the financial repercussions that are inherent in everything that happens to you.

Pavlov is famous for proving that if you brainwash a dog into getting hungry every time you ring a bell, you'll make so much money from this idiotic experiment that it won't bother you at all when the animal rights activists start sending you hate mail for mentally tormenting helpless creatures.

Like Pavlov's dogs, most of us respond predictably (and idiotically) to the stimuli in our environments and, like animal rights activists, we become predictably outraged by senseless behaviors, never stopping to realize that if a dog turns into a salivating zombie whenever an ice cream truck goes down the street, it's not Pavlov's fault — it must be the dog's Karma!

So step back and witness the choices you are making. This act of paying attention to what you are doing takes your choice-making from the unconscious realm to the conscious realm. This should put you into that sacred state the mystics refer to as the Power Trip.

Whenever you make a choice, ask yourself two questions. First, "What are the consequences of this choice?" In your cold, lonely heart, you will know the answer to this. Second, "Will this choice put a little loot into my pockets?" If the answer to this one is yes, then you're probably going to be happy with that choice. If the answer is no, then why are you wasting your time even thinking about it? Get a life.

Of all the choices available to you at any given moment, there is only one choice that will have the biggest financial reward. And when you make that one choice, it is called spontaneous lucrative action. Spontaneous lucrative action is simply making the most profitable decision no matter what the circumstances. It's the choice that gets the bucks flowing in your direction.

There is an interesting mechanism operating in the universe to help you make spontaneously lucrative actions. You must learn to pay attention to subtle sensations in your brain. Your brain experiences two kinds of sensations: one is the sensation of greed, the other is a sensation of compassion. At the moment you are consciously making a choice, pay attention to your brain and ask yourself: "If I make this choice, what happens?" If your brain responds with a greedy laugh, you are making the right choice. If the feeling inside your brain is one of humanitarian compassion, however, then it's not the right choice.

For instance, a homeless beggar approaches you and asks for your spare change. With Pavlovian predictability, you find yourself reaching into your pocket. But stop and ask your brain the two questions you must always ask with every choice you make. One, what are the consequences of this action? The answer to this is obvious: this beggar — obviously a person with really bad Karma — is going to be enriched. Is it your job to enrich the lives of those whose Karma is so bad they have been reduced to begging? And the second question — will this action put a little loot in my pocket? — answers itself! Your choice to enrich the life of someone with bad Karma results in an emptying of your own pockets, thus producing nothing but bad Karma for you!

For some people, the messages of greed and compassion are in the gut, but for most people, they're in the brain. Wherever it is for you, pay attention to it. Ask your brain what to do, and don't proceed until you get the answer. It may be the faintest level of feeling — but it's there, in your brain, in your gut.  You will know the answer.

Most people think their brains are addled and incompetent, but they're not. The brain is smart; it's devious; power hungry; greedy. It doesn't have a good-bad orientation. It taps right into the cosmos — the Field of Pure Greed, pure control, and infinite heartlessness — and quickly assesses the situation. At times, it may seem so cold and uncaring as to be inhuman, but its heartless calculating nature is actually the essence of your humanity; it's far more accurate in its decision-making than the conditioned, predictable, emotional responses which you usually allow to rule your life.

You can use the *Law of Helping Others to Reap Their Bad Karma* to create money and affluence, to become wealthy beyond your wildest dreams, anytime you want. But first, you must become aware that your future results from the choices you make today, at every moment. The more you make your choices according to spontaneous lucrative action, the more you will be utilizing Karma to put bucks into your pocket. And that's what Karma is for.

* * *

What about your past Karma? How does it affect your life today?  When you look at the circumstances of your life — your poverty, your misery, your pent-up frustration, your hopelessness, your desperation, your physical deterioration — your Karmic debts are obviously being paid off slowly but surely. There is a lot of pain and suffering involved in paying off your Karmic debts the way you are unconsciously choosing to do it, but there is a better, painless way to enlightenment.

First of all, worrying about your own past Karma is a waste of time. It's water under the bridge. Obviously, if you're not rich like me, it's because you're paying your Karmic debts. There is a perfect accounting system in this universe; no debt ever goes unpaid.

Sitting around moping about your own predicament, however, gets you nowhere. Do something about it. Whining is useless. The best way to erase your bad Karma, to cleanse the Karmic dirt from your soul, is to stop thinking about yourself and start helping others.

How can I help others, you ask, when I am so desperate myself, when I don't even like people? You ask this question because your definition of "helping others" is predictably shortsighted. Don't be so egotistical. You must realize that you are not the only person on this planet paying Karmic debts. Everyone is paying. You must look for those seeds of opportunity which allow you to be instrumental in helping others to pay their Karmic debts.

For example, if an opportunity arises for you to rip off a business associate, enriching yourself while ruining him financially, you might normally forego this opportunity out of compassion, or friendship, or so-called "business ethics." Ha! There's an oxymoron for you! But this poverty consciousness that guides your actions is not in keeping with spontaneous lucrative action. If, in fact, you are successful in ripping off your associate, then the indisputable fact is: *he deserved it!* It was his Karma. And by helping him spiritually to pay his Karmic debts, you are enriched! You have helped a fellow human being, and the payoff to you is immediate and measurable in dollars and cents.

All actions — no matter how seemingly insignificant — are Karmic episodes. Even drinking a cup of coffee can be a Karmic episode. You could use it to shortchange the waitress! It may seem paradoxical, but anything you do that's "bad" for someone else is actually "good" for them. Helping someone else to reap his or her bad Karma is always a noble act. Likewise, doing something seemingly "good" for someone else is actually "bad." You will just be increasing that person's Karmic debt, and he will pay. Giving money to a beggar is like slapping him in the face.

By becoming a conscious choice-maker, you will begin to generate spontaneous lucrative actions that are truly evolutionary for you and for all those around you. You'll get rich; they'll get poor. The balance of the universe is restored.

# APPLYING THE LAW OF HELPING OTHERS TO REAP THEIR BAD KARMA

I will put the *Law of Helping Others to Reap Their Bad Karma* into effect by making a commitment to take the following steps:

(1) Today I will witness the choices I am making, remembering the story of Pavlov's dogs and the animal rights activists. Senseless cruelty sometimes pays off.

(2) Before I make a choice, I will ask myself: "What are the consequences of this choice," and "Will this choice put money in my pocket?"

(3) I will then ask my brain for guidance, and I will heed its message of greed or compassion. If the choice correlates with my natural greediness, I will plunge ahead with abandon. If I feel instead sappy, human compassion, I will pause and reconsider my action, striving for the spontaneous lucrative action that is more desirable.

# 4

## THE LAW OF GETTING SOMETHING FOR NOTHING

*Nature's intelligence functions with recklessness. Nothing is difficult for nature, because nature doesn't care. A hurricane destroys a village, nature doesn't cry. When you really don't give a damn, you can do anything — even get rich — with reckless ease.*

ã

*Blessed are the meek, for they shall inherit the earth, and we can take it away from them without struggle.*

— *Rev. Jimmy Swaggart*

The fourth spiritual law of making big bucks is the *Law of Getting Something for Nothing.* This law is based on the fact that nature itself operates without morals and without sympathy for its victims. In the end, nature will take all of our lives and reclaim all of our material possessions.

If you observe nature at work, you will see that nature takes everything, giving nothing. Hurricanes don't pay for coastal property. They just destroy it. Wolves don't purchase lambs from the shepherd. They just eat them. Viruses don't pay you rent to live inside your body. They simply invade you. Radiation from the sun doesn't barter with you for a fair price for your healthy cells. It is its intrinsic nature to give you cancer whether you want it or not. It is the nature of babies to selfishly demand attention at all hours of the day and night. We are born demanding little tyrants. It is the nature of black holes to suck in everything in their vicinity. And it is human nature to grab anything and everything desired without paying for it.

In Vedic Science, the age old con game of India, this principle is known as the principle of lazy, good-for-nothing yoga, or "contemplate your navel and get paid for it." Ultimately, you come to be a revered Maharishi, and your mindless followers drive you from one ostentatious ashram to the next in your gold-plated Rolls Royces and your loaded Lincoln Continentals. You do nothing. You say nothing. Your belches are considered messages from God. Baskets of fruit and nubile virgins are laid at your feet for your holy pleasure. This then is the *Law of Getting Something for Nothing.*

Nature's intelligence functions thoughtlessly, cynically, amorally. It is non-caring; it is destructive, painful, and cruel. And when you are in harmony with nature, when you are established in the knowledge of your True Self, you can make use of the *Law of Getting Something for Nothing.*

You activate this law when your actions are motivated by greed, because nature is held together by the energy of greed. When you act compassionately for other people, you violate your greedy nature. When you seek to help others purely for the sake of love and concern for your fellow man, you waste energy chasing the illusion of righteousness instead of enjoying the power you have right now to dominate and control the weak. When you act charitably, with no thought of personal gain, you offend nature's intelligence. But when your actions are motivated by greed and selfishness, there is no waste of energy. With greed motivating you, your energy and your power multiply and accumulate — and the surplus energy you gather and enjoy can be channeled to create anything you want, including unlimited riches.

Think of your physical body as a device for controlling power. It can create, store, and wield unlimited power. If you know how to create and wield power, then you can control and amass money. Caring about other people consumes a great amount of energy. When your internal reference point is concern for others, when your actions are motivated by love and humanitarianism, you waste your power foolishly.

When you free your true power from its unnatural addiction to moralistic insipidness, it can be rechanneled and used to make big bucks. When your internal reference point is your greed, when you are immune to criticism and unfearful of the laws of man, you can harness the power of greed to squash all those who stand in your way.

In The *Art of Scamming,* Louie the Lush tells little Timmy: "... most of our energy goes into giving a shit. If you can just stop giving a shit about what happens to other people, and what other people think about you, or how society might judge your actions, two things would happen. One, you'd stop wasting your time giving a shit about people who don't give a shit about you; and two, your opportunities for ripping people off would skyrocket, because your relatives, your business associates, and your so-called friends would suddenly become fair game."

\* \* \*

There are three components to the *Law of Getting Something for Nothing* — three things you can do to put this principle of "contemplate-your-navel-and-get-paid-for-it" into action. The first component is bitterness. Bitterness simply means that you make a commitment: "Today, I will refuse to accept the sorry sack of crap I have been handed as my lot in life." This means that I will know that at this very moment I am being screwed by the Universe. This moment — the one you are experiencing right now — is the culmination of all the pain you have experienced in the past. This moment is a royal pain in the ass because the entire Universe is a royal pain in the ass.

When you accept this moment as it is, you're actually accepting crap. Instead, you can make the decision that today you will not accept your pathetic excuse for a life. You will bitterly reject everything that happens to you today. This is very important. Be virulently bitter about *everything,* even the most trivial irritations. If the sun is shining, think of skin cancer. If it's raining or snowing, think pneumonia. Always be aware that nature itself is mean and heartless.

If you start to feel warm and generous towards a person, remember that these feelings are unnatural. If someone appears to need your help, your attention, your time, your energy, remember — *it's not your problem.*

Which leads us to the second component of the *Law of Getting Something for Nothing: Irresponsibility.* What does irresponsibility mean? It means blaming anyone else, or any-thing else, for your fucked up existence. By bitterly rejecting your lot at every moment, irresponsibility means that you are free to lash out at everyone around you. All problems contain the seeds of blame, and this awareness allows you to seize the moment and transform it into a moneymaking opportunity at someone else's expense.

Once you do this, every kick in the head will become just another chance for you to put money in the bank, and every friend who "needs" you will become someone you can use and abuse for your own pleasure and enrichment. Reality is a matter of interpretation. If you interpret reality in this way, you will have money sources all around you, and constant op-portunities to increase your net worth at the expense of those surrounding you.

Whenever confronted by any other human being, remind yourself: "This moment sucks." Whatever relationships you have attracted into your life at this time are all people who are trying to get something out of you. You don't need these leeches. Soak them for whatever they're worth, and throw them away. The world's supply of suckers is endless. Their universal purpose is to serve you.

The third component of the *Law of Getting Something for Nothing* is offensiveness, which means that your awareness is in being offensive at all times, and you have relinquished the need to consider anyone else's point of view. If you observe the people around you, you'll see they spend ninety-nine percent of their time trying to convince you that they're right and you're wrong. Fuck 'em. There is no right or wrong. There's my way or the highway.

When you become offensive and take your misery out on other people, the world opens up to you. It's all well and good to piss and moan every time the price of corn flakes goes up at the supermarket, but the sad fact is that Kellogg's doesn't really give a damn about you. Think of how much more productive it is to gouge your own customers and business associates out of a few more of their hard-earned bucks. Go on the offensive! That's the best defense!

When a hungry gazelle meets a hungry tiger in the jungle, two things happen. One, the defenseless gazelle tries to run away. Two, the tiger chases the lunch meat. Sometimes, the gazelle gets away, but one fact remains: tigers eat a hell of a lot more gazelles than gazelles eat tigers!

Stop running away. Start attacking. If you do this consistently — always act on the offensive — you will stop experiencing the present, which is a pain in the ass, and start anticipating the future, which looks a hell of a lot brighter after you've devoured a gazelle or two. A former business partner once told me, "The past was a drain, the present is a pain, so tomorrow I'm getting even." An admirable plan, but stupid. Why wait until tomorrow to get even? There's no time like the present! I cleaned that bastard out that afternoon. If you want to sweeten your tomorrows, the time to attack is *now*.

49

If you live for the future by going on the offensive in the present, you will experience a rush of adrenaline knowing that the world is your oyster. You will know the joy of the eagle as it soars through the skies, its eagle-eyes scanning the terrain below for helpless, but tasty, little critters to feed on. This is the exultation of spirit that you see in the rippling muscles of the lion as it stalks the jungle, always ready to pounce on the weak and unprepared treats that nature has placed in his path. The rush of ecstasy felt by the great white shark, wending its way through the ocean depths, gobbling up little fishes like the sushi smorgasbord they are.

The eagle, the lion, the shark — all realize that the endless feast of life has been provided by nature. This sumptuous repast we call life has been spread before us by the universe. Eat heartily, digest, and eat some more!

In this joyful, simple freedom, you will know, without any doubt in your heart, that you were born to be a glutton at the table of life. You will know that whatever you want is available to you whenever you want it. You do not need to justify your wants; just satisfy them.

The eagle, as it dives towards a scampering titmouse in the field below, does not stop to consider the titmouse's point of view on the matter. The cute little titmouse itself is busy chewing on a spider, which was feasting on a cockroach, which was eating a worm, ad infinitum . . . The eagle swoops, no questions asked, it grabs its prey and flies — the universal amorality of nature: eat or be eaten.

When you stop considering the points of view of others — and only humans do this! — your dreams, your desires, and your reality will flow with nature's desires. When you want, you take. It's that simple. This is the *Law of Getting Something for Nothing*.

# APPLYING THE LAW OF GETTING SOMETHING FOR NOTHING

I will put the *Law of Getting Something for Nothing* into effect by making a commitment to take the following steps:

(1)  I will practice Bitterness. I will refuse to accept my pathetic lot in life. I will know that this moment sucks because the entire Universe sucks. I will be pissed off at everything that happens to me today, knowing that only through dissatisfaction will I realize my destiny.

(2)  Having rejected things as they are, I will practice total Irresponsibility for my actions. I will blame others for my problems, knowing that if others are to blame, others must pay. In this way, I may enrich myself by . . .

(3)  Remaining established at all times in Offensiveness. I will consider no one else's point of view. I really won't give a shit what anyone else might think of me. I'll do what I want, take what I want, and fuck 'em if they can't take a joke.

# ❧ 5 ❧

# THE LAW
# OF NEVER GIVING
# A SUCKER AN
# EVEN BREAK

*Inherent in every one of your grandiose
desires, no matter how bizarre or
embarrassing, is the mechanics for its
fulfillment . . . Desire in the field of pure greed
has infinitely perverse organizing power.
And when we introduce cruelty into the fertile
ground of pure greed, we put this perverse
organizing power to work for us.*

❧

*Modern man is too impatient to seek enlightenment through years of solitary meditation. He tries to find God fast by taking psychoactive drugs. I recommend a gentler path to fulfillment — Jack Daniels.*

*— Meher Babababababaran*

The fifth spiritual law of making big bucks is the *Law of Never Giving a Sucker an Even Break.* This law is based on the fact that the unenlightened masses of humanity are suckers. Phineas T. Barnum seriously underestimated the sucker birth rate. 999 out of 1000 people in this world are born suckers. They have hopes and dreams and attachments to idiotic ideals. They feel love and compassion and profess to various and sundry spiritual beliefs. Misguided, ignorant, illogical, irrational, superstitious jerks, one and all. Join that one-tenth of one percent of the world's population who control their own earthly destiny, and the minions of sheep will follow you as if you were their lord and master. You'll warm yourself in the finest woolen garments, provided by fleecing your starry-eyed flock of worshippers, who will neither notice nor care that you are feasting on mutton burgers every night, while they chew dry grass and dandelions out in your pasture. In fact, they will be ever grateful to you for providing the worthless weeds they subsist on as they provide you with wealth and luxury and a life of lazy pleasure. Let's examine this process in detail.

A flower, a rainbow, a human body, a banana slug, a French poodle, when broken down to their essential components — let's say you put them all together in a giant Cuisinart blender — are just a bunch of sludge that won't smell very good after a few days' time. Everything in the universe, in its essential nature, smells pretty bad when you leave it out of the fridge for a while.

The only difference between you and a tree, on the quantum level, is that you have really bad breath in the morning. On the material level, both you and the tree are composed of the same recycled elements: carbon, hydrogen, oxygen, alcohol, plus various insecticides and preservatives; you've got slightly more caffeine, but the tree edges you out on bird shit — unless, of course, you own a parrot. You could buy most of these elements for a few bucks from any underground drug lab. The real difference between you and the tree, therefore, is not the oxygen or the carbon or even the birdshit; it's the caffeine. Trees don't drink coffee — not because they don't want to, but because they can't operate kitchen appliances.

In the scheme of nature, you and I are a privileged species. We have coffee pots, which allow us to get wired in the morning. Caffeine allows us to experience nervous energy — a feeling a tree cannot relate to at all. Caffeine, in fact, is what separates us from all of the other species on this planet. By all rights, the rulers of this sphere should have been the lions, kings of the jungle. When man became addicted to caffeine, however, in its various forms in various cultures — coffee beans in South America, oolong and green teas in the Orient, Hershey bars in Pennsylvania — man got the survival edge on the predatory cats. Humans woke up in the morning feeling really grouchy, and after a cup of java or two, became conniving bastards, capable of inventing devious, lethal weapons. This is why the ancient seers exclaimed: "My sweet lord, you know I really want to see you, Hare Krishna, Hare Krishna! Where are you, you bastard? I really want to see you, Hare Rama, Hare Rama. Come on out, you coward. Show your face and I'll blow your brains out!"

Not only is the human nervous system on caffeine capable of devising grandiose schemes, it is also capable of maintaining the level of cruelty necessary to carry out these schemes. Caffeine accesses the quantum field, making human consciousness infinitely flexible. When you're wired, you can consciously change the energy and informational content of your quantum mechanical body, and therefore, influence the quantum mechanical body of the universe, or at least, any portion of the universe that dares to get in your way.

This conscious change is brought about by the two qualities inherent in consciousness: craftiness and cruelty. Craftiness energizes and cruelty transforms. Whatever crafty schemes you concentrate on will materialize. Those schemes you ignore will wither and die. Cruelty, on the other hand, triggers the fulfillment of your schemes. If you create a scheme to make a bundle of loot by selling substandard products to an unwary public, it will never come to fruition if you can't actually sell the shoddy merchandise you've stockpiled because you lack the cruelty to unload your crap on your fellow man.

Wake up and smell the coffee.

Literally!

Let's say you've got a warehouse full of adult diapers you purchased from a factory in Taiwan. The box says "Depends." They look like Depends, but they're not Depends. They're Depends knockoffs, made by the same company that produces those $15.00 "Rolex" watches. There are two major differences between your phony Depends and the real thing. One, real Depends will cost you about a buck-fifty a box wholesale; fake Depends cost a nickel a gross. And two, unfortunately, fake Depends leak. Fast. Real fast.

If you stop and think about your favorite Aunt Melba, who used to bring you Snickers bars and take you to the park for merry-go-round rides, but who now lives in a rest home, uses a walker, and wears adult diapers, you'll never be able to sell your substandard merchandise.

Here's what to do:

Forget about Aunt Melba. Have a cup of coffee, then have another one, and another. In the scheme of nature, nothing actually correlates or connects with anything else. It's all illusion, maya, a surrealistic cosmic dream.

What is remarkable about the nervous system of the human species is that it can command this dream to go wherever it wants to go. So, why should you go back decades to remember your Aunt Melba if this interferes with your carefully crafted scheme to get rich?

Think instead of Elvis Presley. Remember Elvis, that obese hillbilly, drugged out, space cadet who had more kinky sex on any given weekend than the Marquis de Sade in his prime? Elvis was incontinent. He depended on Depends (or, more likely, some outrageously expensive designer brand of adult diaper — maybe "Chanel Repels" or "Bill Blass for Your Ass"). Now think of Elvis on stage in Vegas, in his trademark rhinestone-studded jumpsuit, middle-aged women screaming and drooling and fainting in the aisles. And the King is about to discover, right there under the spotlight, that he's wearing Taiwanese knockoff Depends, all over his blue suede shoes!

Kind of gets you chuckling, doesn't it? Have another cup of java, then get out there and unload your warehouseful of laughs on the local Safeway buyer, that greedy S.O.B., who thinks he's saving a few pennies for the company — probably skimming half the profits into his own pockets — by taking a shipment from you instead of Proctor and Gamble (or whoever the hell makes real Depends).

Cruelty — the ability to laugh gleefully at the misfortune of others — combined with craftiness, leads to wealth-centered awareness. And when any action is performed with wealth-centered awareness, you make bucks. In other words, as long as you do not violate the other laws of nature, through your cruelty, you can literally command the laws of nature to fulfill your wickedest dreams and desires, and you'll provide yourself with a lot of laughs in the process.

You can put the cosmic computer with its infinitely perverse organizing power to work for you. Just being mean doesn't do it. True cruelty is the ability to find joy and happiness in the misfortunes of others. This happens spontaneously when you are in alignment with the Seven Spiritual Laws of Making Big Bucks.

\* \* \*

Craftiness is the real power behind greed. Craftiness alone is very powerful because craftiness is greed without caring about who gets hurt. Greed alone is weak because greed does not preclude compassion. Craftiness is born of greed combined with strict adherence to the *Law of Detachment, or Perfect Heartlessness,* which is the Sixth Spiritual Law of Making Big Bucks.

Craftiness combined with Perfect Heartlessness leads to wealth-centered awareness. You are crafty when plotting your future net worth, but your devious schemes must be carried out in the present. As long as you follow through with your schemes today, then the future of wealth you have crafted will manifest itself because the future is created in the present.

The past, present and future are all properties of God's incompetence. If God really had his act together, he would have created one, perfect, ecstatic moment in time. Instead, we get this shitty drudgery that we call "life." Most people — no matter what label they put on their "religion" — think of God as all-knowing, all-powerful, and all-loving.

What a crock! Think about it for a second . . . If God knew everything, does he not know there are millions of starving children in this world? If he's omnipotent, doesn't he have the power to feed them? If he's so all-loving, why does he just let them die in pain and despair?

The fact is, God is an incompetent, mean son-of-a-bitch who knows very little about what's happening and who cares even less, as is apparent if you just look at this poor excuse for a Universe he's created.

Most humans delude themselves into believing that God is this mighty and wonderful Master of Creation, worthy of praise and worship. Why not be honest with yourself and just admit it: The Cosmic Asshole fucked up! This God we got stuck with as our creator has serious mental deficiencies. We were created by a heartless idiot! That's the one, irrefutable, cosmic truth that none of our sanctimonious religious "leaders" tell us.

Some people, using a few more brain cells than the masses, see the utter chaos of creation, the pain, the torture, the suffering, the catastrophes, the disease, the wars, the hatred, and the inevitable death of all, and they profess atheism.

"There is no God," they say bluntly, with a feeling of superiority over the misguided churchgoers. The fact is atheists are cowards. They see the horror of life, but they refuse to acknowledge that this cosmic shitstorm could have been created by a God as incompetent and downright nasty as this God would have to be! Most of these so-called atheists reject the concept of God because they perceive themselves as more loving, more compassionate and frankly smarter than any God who would have created this sorry universe. So, they surmise, God doesn't exist. Atheists, in fact, are a bunch of humanitarian do-gooders who believe in political "solutions," and scientific "solutions," and social "solutions." They really believe something will eventually "solve" this mess.

Again I say, wake up and smell the coffee. Unfortunately, there is a God, and this world we live in really is the best he could do. And if you really believe you can do better than the jerk who created you, you're as bad off as the mindless suckers who worship him!

Learn to harness the power of *Law of Never Giving a Sucker an Even Break* (does God give anyone an even break?), and you will realize your true, Godlike nature —

you're incompetent, you're mean, and you don't care. When you follow these five steps for fulfilling your desires, your craftiness generates its own power:

(1) Have a cup of coffee. Strong coffee. Slip into that silent space between your thoughts, that wired level of Being which is your true state of reality.

(2) Established in that state of Being, start scheming. Write down your desires, no matter how perverse or outlandish they may be.

(3) Discuss the criminal implications with your attorney. If your attorney has "moral" objections, he's probably an atheist (few attorneys believe in God); get another attorney.

(4) Relinquish your attachment to the outcome. Forget about who might get hurt. Does God worry about who might get hurt when he creates a hurricane? No, he just sits back on a comfy cloud, eating popcorn, watching the wind blow, trees being uprooted, homes being destroyed, until he tires of it and "switches the channel," so he can watch the famine he's created in some underdeveloped third world country.

(5) Have another cup of coffee.

# APPLYING THE LAW OF NEVER GIVING A SUCKER AN EVEN BREAK

I will put the *Law of Never Giving a Sucker an Even Break* into effect by making a commitment to take the following steps:

(1) I will make a list of all my darkest desires. I will not carry this list with me, in case I am ever searched by the police. I will hide the list in a safe place.

(2) I will commit the list of my desires to my memory, trusting that when things don't go my way, I will find some devious way to make somebody else pay for my misfortune.

(3) I will buy stock in Starbucks.

# ❧ 6 ❧

# THE LAW
# OF TOTAL
# DETACHMENT,
# OR PERFECT
# HEARTLESSNESS

*In detachment lies the wisdom of neglect —
freedom from stress, and from peer pressure.
In our willingness to neglect our so-called
"responsibilities," we surrender ourselves to
the conniving cosmic mind that orchestrates
this grand catastrophe we call existence,
and we quietly rake in the loot.*

༄

*So, what's it to you?*

— *Maharishi Mahesh Bundy*

The sixth spiritual law of making big bucks is the *Law of Total Detachment, or Perfect Heartlessness.* The *Law of Total Detachment* says that in order to acquire anything in the physical universe, you have to relinquish your attachment to the sonofabitch who currently owns it. This doesn't mean you give up your relationship with that person, assuming you have one. You give up your *attachment* to that person.

The very word "attachment" means to be attached, or connected, to someone or something. Attachment also implies involuntary connection. If I am handcuffed to someone, I am attached to that person. If I am bound to a tree with a length of rope, I am attached to that tree. To be attached to anyone or anything is always unpleasant, as our personal freedom has been restricted.

On the other hand, if I have a dog on a leash, we would not say I am attached to the dog, as my connection to that dog is one that I control, and one that I may relinquish at any time. If I have a puppet on a string, I am not attached to that puppet. My connection to that puppet is one that I purposefully hold onto. I am the one who pulls the strings. The puppet does not pull my strings as I have no strings, no attachments which allow me to be manipulated.

In the literal sense — unless at this moment you happen to be either handcuffed to a police officer or enjoying an evening at your local bondage studio — you are not attached to anyone or anything. Yet, you live under the delusion that you have multiple attachments — to people, places, objects, activities. You have created in your mind a hundred invisible strings which you allow the world around you to pull. You are but a puppet in the punch-and-Judy show of your life. And until you realize that these invisible strings are simply a figment of your own imagination, you will feel attachment. The only actual attachment you have is to these imaginary strings.

When you put your dog on the leash and take him for a walk around the block, you are not attached to the dog, yet the dog is attached to you. He cannot follow his own will. He must go where you go, at your pace.

If your dog is properly trained, you do not even need the leash. Having established yourself as the master, your dog is forever "attached" to you. He will never be free again to follow his own path, to explore the world at his whim. He believes his attachment to you is real. He will never run free, despite the fact that he could easily outrun you.

Are you a puppet? Are you a dog? The leash that pulls you, the strings that restrict the direction and pace of your life, are but figments of your imagination. Mentally, you must unleash yourself from your attachments, cut those strings that pull you.

This is a very powerful thing to do. The moment you relinquish your attachment to those people you have relationships with, you may fleece them freely because detachment is based on your unquestioning belief in your right to do what you want.

Attachment, on the other hand, is based on fear, insecurity and caring about people. Caring about people is based on the Cosmic Lie that you need other people and that other people care about you. The Cosmic Truth is that you need nothing and no one; you are complete in yourself. And it's a good thing you are because no one really gives a hairy Krishna about you.

True wealth consciousness is the ability to have anything and anyone you want, anytime you want, for your personal pleasure. Whenever you find yourself deluding yourself into believing that other people care about you and need you, remember the Donner Party. When it all comes down to "eat or be eaten," we all say, ever so politely, "Excuse me, but could you please pass the Grey Poupon?"

People are constantly seeking security. You might say, "When I have 100 million dollars, I'll be happy. I'll retire. I'll travel. I'll eat like a king, and do what I want. I'll have servants and chauffeurs and upstairs maids in frilly lingerie, a Lear jet, a private island in the Caribbean, movie stars for friends." And it's true that this is how you would live if you had 100 million dollars — and I am speaking from experience because this is how I live! But for you, it never happens — never happens!

Why? Because you retain your attachments to the unenlightened fools who surround you. They pull your invisible strings and you move this way and that way at their bidding, smiling all along like Howdy Doody, unable to wipe that wooden grin off your face. You follow the formulated script of your life exactly as written by those who use you to satisfy their own insecurities.

If you relinquish your attachment to those with whom you interact, you will step into the field of heartlessness. And in your willingness to step into the field of heartlessness, to become a person with no strings attached, you will suddenly become aware of the invisible strings attached to all those you encounter. You may pull those strings at your whim, as you become the puppet master of your own life.

One characteristic of the field of heartlessness is infinite apathy. In the same way that the universe itself cares nothing about what happens to this planet we call Earth, this little speck of wet dirt in the cosmos, you will find when you free yourself from your attachments that you will see your fellow humans simply for what they are — meat with an attitude.

The so-called "plight of man" is an egotistical delusion of this silly, minor species that, incredibly, believes in its moral superiority over other life forms.

Moral superiority my ass.

Blind arrogance!

All around us the astounding miracle of existence unfolds. We close our eyes and pound our chests and proclaim our self-importance. God himself, the incompetent designer of this grand catastrophe, doesn't even bother to chuckle at our stupidity. The Heavenly Cretin is too busy picking his holy nose, flinging boogers at the stars. It's just a game with him, a way to pass the time. The cosmos is his giant pinball game. He extinguishes a solar system here, slimes a galaxy there, all the while trying to dodge the black holes.

*The Law of Total Detachment, or Perfect Heartlessness,* accelerates your evolution to the highest plane of consciousness, the Apathy of God. Every problem you have in your life solves itself when you relinquish your moral superiority, because once you let go of your moral superiority, you will stop seeking moral solutions. The concepts of good and evil, which you hold so dear, are but illusions, two sides of the same coin. All the great mystics have discovered this truth. By limiting yourself to what you perceive as the "good" solutions to your problems, you discard at least half of the potential opportunities to solve your problems. You ignore all of the so-called "evil" solutions, and you call that your "moral superiority." I call it your "flock mentality." You are a sheep, bleating your way through life. I am the shepherd, and I shall fleece you without a moral qualm!

Welcome to my pasture!

# Applying the Law of Total Detachment or Perfect Heartlessness

I will put the *Law of Total Detachment, or Perfect Heartlessness,* into effect by making a commitment to take the following steps:

(1) Today, I will commit myself to detached behavior. When a problem presents itself, I will seek solutions, and not just "good" solutions. I will relinquish my belief in man's moral superiority, knowing that the concepts of "good" and "evil" are fictitious.

(2) Today, I will factor in heartlessness as a necessary ingredient of my life. The more heartless I perceive myself to be, the more secure I will feel that I am realizing my true Godlike nature — uncaring incompetence.

(3) I will consciously relinquish the invisible strings that allow others to yank me from the heartless path of my life. And as my own strings disappear, I will begin to see the strings attached to those around me. All those whom I encounter shall be like puppets in a slapstick comedy that I direct for my own entertainment.

# 7

# THE LAW OF WALLOWING IN WEIRDNESS

*Everyone thinks there is a purpose in life, a reason to go on despite the horrors of existence. Everyone is wrong.*
*There is no purpose to life other than for the amusement of a heartless God. Our Creator has no grand plan for us. This is it.*

❧

*All is holy. All is sacred. Every place a temple. Every word a prayer. Every thought a creation of the One. Got a match? My ass and your face!*

*— Lao Bao Wao*

The seventh spiritual law of making big bucks is the *Law of Wallowing in Weirdness*. "Wallow" comes from a Sanskrit word which means "Godlike indolence." The *Law of Wallowing in Weirdness* says that we have taken manifestation in physical form to be like God — lazy, good-for-nothing weirdos. The field of pure greed is divinity in essence, and the divine takes human form in order to experience more bizarre and meaningless pleasure.

According to this law, you have a unique talent for sloth, and a unique way of experiencing aberrant pleasure. There is some form of depravity that satisfies your natural selfishness more than anyone else in the world — and for every unique pleasure, there is a pervert willing to accommodate you. I don't care how bizarre your desires are, believe me, there is someone who will not only cater to your whims, but *pay you for the privilege of satisfying you!*

In fact, the more outrageous your desires, the easier it is to get them fulfilled! People with money will pay you to abuse them. Most Americans, when they want a housekeeper, look for illegal aliens who are willing to scrub floors, wash pots, and clean toilets for less than the minimum wage paid under the table. But it is sheer idiocy to ever pay anyone any of your hard-earned cash to perform these menial tasks.

Many bankers, CEO's, and high-powered corporate attorneys are more than happy to pay you big bucks to treat them like servants and slaves. They will grovel at your feet for the sacred honor of scouring your shower stall with a toothbrush in a Brooks Brothers suit, fashionably accessorized with a studded dog collar.

Even as I write these words, the fat and balding president of a Fortune 500 company is prancing around my living room in a tutu, dusting my knickknack shelves; a local TV weatherman, bare-assed in leather chaps and nipple-clamps, is painting my garage; and the trophy wife of the my esteemed Congressman is tied up with duct tape in my den, as she waits for me to arrive with the riding crop, the goat, the WD-40, the Jell-O Pudding Pops, and the catcher's mitt. All are *paying me* for exploiting *their* depraved fantasies. These people are not unusual. The fact is, deep down, everyone's a weirdo.

If you could start your children right from the start with this thought, you would see the effect it has on their lives. In fact, I did this with my own children. Repeatedly, I told them there was no good reason for their existence on this planet, that God was an incompetent idiot, and that nothing would be given to them. "If you want anything in this world," I often said, "then get your astral ass in gear and take it. Never worry about making a contribution to society. Those who contribute are the worker ants who sweat and slave their pathetic lives away. Be like me. Do less and accomplish more. Don't worry about studying in school. Learn to cheat. It'll help you later in life when it comes time to pay your taxes. What I really want you to focus on is manipulating people into doing things for you and giving you things. You have strange desires, and only you know what gets you off. Go for it."

At the age of 14, my son ran away from home, after stealing my television and cleaning out my wallet. What a kid! Today, he's a televangelist, making more tax-free money in a week than I make in a year. My daughter, bless her heart, has followed in my footsteps to become a writer. After five years in the porno industry, she landed an editorial job in New York. The seven-digit advance she garnered for her soon-to-be-published unauthorized biography of Mother Theresa, *Twisted Sister* — which exposes the late nun as a vicious serial killer — has already locked Geraldo and Oprah in a bidding war for her talk show debut. What a kid!

There are three components to the *Law of Wallowing in Weirdness*. The first component says that each of us is here to discover our Abnormal Nature. We are not normal beings who have occasional weird experiences. We are weirdoes who have occasional normal experiences.

The second component of the *Law of Wallowing in Weirdness* requires that after we discover our unique weirdness, we make an effort to express it. Though you might prefer to deny it, you have a perversion that is so freakish in its expression that most of the people on this planet would lock you up and throw away the key if they knew you were even thinking about it. There is one truly nasty fantasy that is yours alone, and when you are lost in that slimy reverie, you lose all track of time. Since we know that time is an illusion, we must recognize this dark fantasy as our quickest route into our disgusting spiritual nature. And don't pretend that you don't know the fantasy I'm referring to; it's the one that consumes the secret moments of your life, the one that would reduce you to shame and embarrassment and denial if ever revealed. Yes, that one.

The third component of the *Law of Wallowing in Weirdness* is mastery over other humans — specifically, getting your fellow humans to ask: "How may I serve you?" When you combine your unique perversion with mastery over those who would fulfill your degenerate desires, you make full use of the *Law of Wallowing in Weirdness.*

To put it succinctly, every person knows he is a weirdo down deep, but believes that other people are normal. Because the unenlightened masses harbor this Hidden Core of Shame, you can manipulate them into paying you for satisfying their innermost desires; and, at the same time, they will pay you to satisfy your desires. When you have no shame, you collect on both ends!

The question people always ask, "How can I help?" is the insipid dialogue of the unenlightened mind. "What's in it for me?" is the honest dialogue of your soul. In shifting your internal dialogue from "How can I help?" to "What's in it for me?" you automatically go into your true greedy nature.

If you want to make maximum use of the *Law of Wallowing in Weirdness,* you must honestly answer two questions: (1) If others' opinions of you were of no concern, what would you be doing? If you would still be living exactly as you are now living (fat chance!), then you are already wallowing in your weirdness. (2) How do I want others to serve me? Answer that, and go for it!

Acknowledge your selfishness, find your unique perversion, use others for your pleasure, and make them pay you for the privilege. Do all of these things and you will begin to experience your life as a Divine Hedonistic Weirdo. You will know the true joy and ecstasy of the mystics.

# APPLYING THE LAW OF WALLOWING IN WEIRDNESS, OR THE PURPOSE OF LIFE

I will put the *Law of Wallowing in Weirdness* into effect by making a commitment to take the following steps:

(1) Today I will enthusiastically embrace my Abnormal Nature as my personal path to Wisdom, allowing myself to fall into that state of Being where time ceases to exist.

(2) In this state, I will make a list of my most bizarre fantasies, knowing that only by entertaining my perversions am I true to my Godlike hedonistic nature.

(3) I will ask myself each day, "What's in it for me?" The answer to this question is: money, fun, power, more money, more fun, and more power, as I joyously exploit the weirdness of others and make them pay for the privilege of satisfying me.

∂

# Summary and Conclusion

*Spare change?*
*— Gautama Buddha*

S ince the dawn of creation, our heartless God, in his infinite incompetence, has neglected and abandoned us to a
useless existence of pain and suffering. For each of us, this
meaningless earthly journey will end in death. The human
body, born in pain through the mother's torturous agony of
birth, is the most perfect example of God's incompetence.

We are all born screaming, hungry, wanting, weak, unable to take care of ourselves, vulnerable to a thousand dis-
eases and malfunctions — God's cynical idea of a creature
fashioned in his own likeness.

Every cell of the human body — whether it's a stomach
cell, or a lung cell, or a brain cell — follows by nature the *Law
of Pure Greed.* The stomach cries for food, the lungs for oxygen, the brain for myriad comforts and pleasures. The skin
cries for warmth, the tongue for delectable flavors, the eyes
for visions of loveliness, the ears for music, and on and on.

Our history as a creature on this planet has been one of constant fighting and killing, raping and stealing, genocide and destruction. It is our nature to take that which our God has created us to want. But only through adherence to the *Seven Spiritual Laws of Making Big Bucks* can we do like God does — get everything we want despite our lazy incompetence. If you pay attention to the steps outlined in this book, you too can get rich like me. These are the same principles followed by every wealthy holy man since time began. Be a bastard, make a bundle.

You can remember these laws by considering the ways in which they naturally relate to each other. The *Law of Pure Greed* is experienced through prejudging others to be conniving SOB's, then silently stewing in anger and resentment over your pathetic lot in life, but it is activated through the *Law of Taking.* This law instructs you to take what you want, giving nothing in return. By practicing this law rigorously, you then activate the *Law of Helping Others to Reap Their Bad Karma.* When you help others to pay their Karmic debts, it will inevitably enrich you, which automatically activates the *Law of Getting Something for Nothing.* When the bucks start rolling in, this in turn activates the *Law of Never Giving a Sucker an Even Break.* This cosmic Power Trip ultimately activates the *Law of Total Detachment, or Perfect Heartlessness,* because you can't exploit all the suckers in this world unless you possess the heartlessness of God. And this total detachment from any feelings for your fellow man activates the *Law of*

*Wallowing in Weirdness.* When you finally have the big bank-roll, you can do what you want, when you want, to whomever you want, without a care. Like God, you will know the meaning of blissful indolence and perversity.

Most people believe they are travelers on a cosmic journey. What a crock; they ain't going nowhere. Time and space are but illusions, created for the sick entertainment of a bored and depraved Deity. This universe at this very moment is right where it always has been, and right where it always will be. And it sucks. The mystics know this.

But since the "cosmic travelers" think they're heading somewhere, it's not our job to disabuse them of this notion. No, it's much more profitable to stop traveling and become an innkeeper at the side of the road. Open a motel, a restaurant, a casino, a movie theater, a church, a bank, a sushi bar, a bowling alley, a school, a brothel, a law office, a self-help seminar. Make those weary travelers pay by the mile.

We have stopped for a moment on this journey to nowhere to put a few more bucks in my pocket. Thanks for buying this book. I hope you've learned something. As in all of our cosmic meetings, whether through my books, my tapes, or my seminars, you pay the money, and I take it home. Perhaps you'll hear my cosmic laughter ringing all the way to the bank. . .

᷐

# ABOUT THE AUTHOR

**D**eepockets Chokya is the reviled leader of the human impotential movement. He is the pseudonymous hack writer of more than eleven hundred worthless pamphlets on how to get rich quick, pick up girls, lose weight, cure cancer, clear your sinuses, get rid of your acne, grow hair, make your cellulite disappear, enlarge your penis, enhance your breasts, increase your vocabulary, and be immortal. Some of his best-selling titles include: *Swindling the Elderly, How to Hypnotize Total Strangers to Do Your Bidding,* and *Creative Flatulence.* Wanted in twelve states for fraud, he continues to flaunt the law by regularly appearing on TV talk shows and teaching seminars on how to pay off judges when you're in trouble with the postal inspectors.

❧

**T**he Seven Spiritual Laws of Making Big Bucks form the essence of *Creative Flatulence: Turning Your Hot Air Into Hard Cash.* In this remarkable excuse for a book, Deepockets Chokya explores the full meaning of mystical mumbo-jumbo and presents a series of simple A-to-Z steps and everyday actions that spontaneously generate huge piles of cash in unmarked bills.

*Creative Flatulence* is available in a tremendously overpriced hard cover edition, destined to be forgotten on your bookshelves along with all the other nonsensical self-help books you've purchased through the years in your vain attempt to find meaning in your dismal life.

## Also Available in Audio Cassette:

*The Seven Spiritual Laws of Ponzi Schemes*
*The Eight Spiritual Laws of Three-Card Monte*
*The Nine Spiritual Laws of Skipping Town Without a Trace*

~

# ABOUT THE REAL AUTHOR

**D**eepockets Chokya is the pseudonym of Thom Hover, an Oakland, California, writer who — although born and raised in Detroit, Michigan — primarily developed his bad attitude through 23 years in the U.S. Postal Service. He quit his job as a letter carrier in 1993. He says:

"When I lived in Detroit, it was known as the Murder Capital of the country. Then, after I moved to Oakland, Oakland became known as the Murder Capital. Honestly, this was just a coincidence. But my years with the Post Office had left me feeling . . . disgruntled. Life seemed to offer only three logical choices: (1) get an Uzi; (2) get an AK-47; or (3) write this book.

"Although Uzis and AK-47s are easily available on the streets of Oakland, writing this book just struck me as a more spiritual way to express my creative rage. And isn't that what life's about?"

email: hover@rge21.com